Princeton University Class of 1896

Record of the Class of 1896 of Princeton University

Number One

Princeton University Class of 1896

Record of the Class of 1896 of Princeton University
Number One

ISBN/EAN: 9783337172800

Printed in Europe, USA, Canada, Australia, Japan

Cover: Foto ©ninafisch / pixelio.de

More available books at **www.hansebooks.com**

Record of the
Class of 1896 of
Princeton University

Number One
April first, 1898

Class Officers.

ALBERT GOODSELL MILBANK, *President,*
No. 42 West Thirty-eighth Street,
New York City.

CHARLES BYRON BOSTWICK, *Secretary,*
No. 324 West Forty-sixth Street,
New York City.

To the Class.

❦

THIS little bundle of facts, that staggers under the dignified title of "Class Record," is offered to the friends and members of Ninety Six in an endeavor to fill a dual need. The primary and paramount motive of its publication is the hope that it may be one more link that binds us together in class union as loyal Princeton men; and if it serves this purpose the labor preceding its issue has not been wasted. It also aims to satisfy a further practical need by enabling both the members of the class and all interested fellow Princetonians to know where any particular man is to be found, and what Ninety Six men are residing in or near our large cities, where it is often necessary to gather Princeton men together. The many requests for just this kind of information that have been addressed to the class secretary during the past year are a good index of the desirability of having it in printed form.

It has been the earnest endeavor of your secretary to have this little book give the latest information about each man, and to have the absence of errors a distinguishing feature. In theory this is delightfully possible, but the practical results will, I fear, be found unsatisfactory in many cases. The effectiveness of graduate organization largely depends upon the promptness and reliability of the individual members in responding to class correspondence, and upon their faithfulness in keeping the secretary advised of their changes of residence and occupation; but it seems that this foundation, being only human, is too often unstable. And, as there has not yet been discovered any subtle mental process whereby we can know of the lives of absent friends without either direct or indirect communication with

4

them, paucity of information will often result in misstatement. So if the following information about yourselves is incomplete or out of date, it will undoubtedly be found that the cause is your own failure to write.

During the Christmas holidays this winter I was talking with a Ninety Six man whom I had not seen since graduation, and as the course of conversation drifted toward class matters, he said, speaking of my letters to the class: "Why, you don't expect us to answer those things, do you?" This, coming from a "rooter of the rooters," was rather staggering. And, judging from facts, it seems to be the attitude of not a few, who were most prominent in college, and of whose devotion to the Alma Mater there is no doubt. Against such opinions the most painstaking efforts of your secretary can be of little avail; but, fortunately, those who profess this heresy are in the distinguished minority. The larger part of the class are prompt in their responses, and much praise is due them for their efforts to strengthen our union. I trust it is not out of place here, if I allow the personal element to enter for a moment, in extending my heartiest thanks to those men on whom I can always count for an immediate response to the class letters.

With these few words of introduction the First Class Record is offered to the Class of Ninety Six, in the hope that its shortcomings will be overlooked upon consideration of the many hours of leisure that have been sacrificed in its preparation, and of the excellence of the motives that have prompted its issue.

C. B. BOSTWICK.

No. 324 West 46th St., New York City,
March 15, 1898.

Roll of Membership.

Explanatory.

Names of ex-members are printed with an asterisk (*) following. Where two addresses are given, the second is that of temporary residence.

Unless otherwise stated, the degrees affixed to the members' names denote those conferred at graduation, June 10, 1896.

Charles Edward Adams,* A. B. (Univ. of Minn., '96).
923 8th St., S. E., Minneapolis, Minn.
Superintendent Public Schools, Granite Falls, Minn. Reading Law.
Expects to enter University of Minnesota Law School in fall
of 1898.

Hugh Clairborne Adams.*
916 N. Garrison Ave., St. Louis, Mo. ; 267 Merchants' Exchange.
St. Louis, Mo.
Grain Broker.

Joseph Warren Alford.*
89 Harrison St., East Orange, N. J. ; 195 Broadway, New York,
Treasurer of " The C. G. Alford Co.," Wholesale Jewelers.

Francis Olcott Allen, Jr., A. B.
1539 Pine St., Philadelphia, Pa.
Studying Medicine at University of Pennsylvania.

6

George Klots Allen, Jr., C. E.

Red Bank, N. J.

Lumber and Hardware Business, Red Bank, N. J.

Harry McClellan Anderson.*

Charleston, W. Va.; Center College, Danville, Ky.

Studying Law.

Henry Beard Armes, A. B.

15th St. and Kenesaw Ave., Washington, D. C.

Studying at Columbian University Law School.

William Mayo Atkinson, A. B.

458 Jefferson Ave., Elizabeth, N. J.

Studying at New York Law School.

Frank Allen Baker, A. B.

914 Cherry St., Kansas City, Mo.

With "Ridenour-Baker Grocery Co.," Kansas City, Mo.

Hugh Wilson Barnett, B. S.

239 N. Limestone St., Springfield, O.

With "Billow & Barnett," Fire Insurance, 25 Bushnell Building, Springfield, O.

Mason Brown Barret, A. B.

1714 Brook St., Louisville, Ky.; 414 Center St., Louisville, Ky.

Attorney-at-Law.

William S. Baylis.

Englewood, N. J.

With "Provident Savings Life Assurance Society," New York.

Jacob Newton Beam, A. B.

Intercourse, Pa.; Princeton, N. J.

Instructor at "Princeton Preparatory School."

Erasmus Bennett, Jr.*

801 Buchanan St., Topeka Kan.

Henry Hannah Bergen.

31 Strong Place, Brooklyn, N. Y.

7

Andrew Jefferson Berry, A. B.
466 Grier St., Augusta, Ga.

Edward Hodge Bishop, A. B.
20 Burnett St., East Orange, N. J.; Easton, Md.
Teaching in Maryland Nautical Academy, Easton, Md.

Amos Bissell.*
Milford, N. Y.; 85 Humboldt Ave., Roxbury, Mass.
With "Horace Partridge Co.,"Athletic Outfitters, 55 Hanover St.,
    Boston, Mass.

George Glover Blackmore, C. E.
3122 Woodburn Ave., Cincinnati, Ohio; 127 West 48th St., New
    York.
Engineering, "Metropolitan Street Railway Co.," New York.

Edgar Thomas Blackwell, C. E.
P. O. Box 86, Hopewell, N. J.; 88 Nassau St., Princeton, N. J.
Studying at Princeton University.

Harry William Bloch.
922 South 18th St., Philadelphia, Pa.; Princeton, N. J.
Studying at Princeton Theological Seminary.

Parker Johnson Boice.*
275 North Delaware St., Indianapolis, Ind.

Charles Byron Bostwick, A. B.
324 West 46th St., New York; P. O. Box 787, New York.
With "Provident Savings Life Assurance Society," New York.

Lawrance Foster Bower, A. B.
116 Dithridge St., Pittsburg, Pa.; Chelsea Square, New York.
Studying at General Theological Seminary, New York City.

John Isaac Bowes.*
325 North Highland Ave., Pittsburg, Pa.; 15 East Otterman St.,
    Greensburg, Pa.

Carl Miner Bowman, A. B.
1814 North Broad St., Philadelphia, Pa.
Studying Law at the University of Pennsylvania.

Robert Walter Brace, A. B.
Blackwood, N. J.
Studying at Medical and Chirurgical College, Philadelphia, Pa.

Edward Swayne Brearley, A. B.
Lawrenceville, N. J.; 62 Brown Hall Seminary, Princeton, N. J.
Studying at Princeton Theological Seminary.

Charles Oscar Bressler, A. B.
55 North 4th St., Lebanon, Pa.
Reading Law in office of Grant Weidman, Jr., 1914 9th St., Lebanon, Pa.

Milner Brien, A. B.
34 Central Ave., Dayton, Ohio; Room 5, Callahan Building, Dayton, Ohio.
Agent New York Life Insurance Co.

Bernis Brien.
34 Central Ave., Dayton, Ohio.
Journalist, "Dayton Evening Journal."

Henry Clay Briggs, A. B.
202 Ross St , Brooklyn, N. Y.; Princeton, N. J.
Studying at Princeton Theological Seminary; also Organist in First Reformed Church of Brooklyn (Bedford Ave.).

Robert Ormiston Brockway.*
13 Greene Ave., Brooklyn, N. Y.
Doing nothing when last heard from.

Edwin Henry Bronson, A. B.
3845 Haverford Ave., Philadelphia, Pa.; Princeton, N. J.
Studying at Princeton Theological Seminary.

Macy Brooks, A. B.
117 North 33d St., Philadelphia, Pa.
Studying Medicine at University of Pennsylvania.

Arthur Houston Brown, C. E.
1208 Delaware St., Lawrence, Kan.; Princeton, N. J.
Studying Electrical Engineering at Princeton University.

Oscar Irwin Brown.[*]
250 West 42d St., New York.
Civil Engineer, Erie Railroad Co.

Charles Browne, A. B.
1126 Spruce St., Philadelphia, Pa.
Studying Medicine at University of Pennsylvania.

Henry Munro Bruen, A. B.
Belvidere, N. J.; 41 East 69th St., New York.
Studying at Union Theological Seminary.

James Bayley Bruen, A. B.
Belvidere, N. J.; care of A. Q. Keasbey & Sons, Prudential Building, Newark, N. J.
Studying at New York Law School and Reading Law in offices of A. Q. Keasbey & Sons, Newark, N. J.

William Bush, B. S.
1208 Delaware Ave., Wilmington, Del.; Room 205, Equitable Building, Wilmington, Del.
Reading Law.

Roderick Byington, Jr., B. S.
150 West 66th St., New York.
Studying at College of Physicians and Surgeons, New York.

Thomas Cadwalader, A. B.
Fort Washington, Pa.; Franklin Building, Philadelphia, Pa.
Studying at University of Pennsylvania Law School.

John McDowell Carnochan.
205 Pine St., Towanda, Pa.
Studying at Medical and Chirurgical College, Philadelphia, Pa.

Pierce Annesley Chamberlain, A. B.[*]
Bahia, Brazil; 1060 North Halstead St., Chicago, Ill.
Studying at McCormick Theological Seminary.

Walter Chandler, Jr., B. S.
583 Newark Ave., Elizabeth, N. J.
With "R. C. Rathbone & Son," Fire Insurance, 27 Pine St., New York.

10

Philip Hudson Churchman, A. B.
18 West Union St., Burlington, N. J.; 37 Gravers Lane, Chestnut Hill, Pa.
Instructor in "Chestnut Hill Academy."

Luther Stowell Clark.*
566 Scotland St., Orange, N. J.
With "Blake Brothers & Co.," Bankers, 5 Nassau St., New York.

Brutus Junius Clay, Jr., A. B.
Paris, Ky.
Studying Law at University of Virginia, Charlottesville, Va.

James Blair Cochran, A. B.
550 Park Ave., New York.
Studying at Union Theological Seminary, 41 East 69th St., New York.

Theodore Clifford Coe, A. B.
45 South 12th St., Newark, N. J.
Studying Law.

Logan Coleman, B. S.
Springfield, Ill.

Thornton Conover.*
Bayard Ave., Princeton, N. J.
With Burton Bros. & Co., Wholesale Dry Goods, 384 Broadway, New York.

John Bliss Corser.*
25 North Centre St., Pottsville, Pa.; 3328 Walnut St., Philadelphia, Pa.
Studying Medicine at University of Pennsylvania.

Henry Welty Coulter, A. B.
Greensburg, Pa.
With "First National Bank," Greensburg, Pa.

Josiah Hughes Crawford, A. B.
Temporary Address: 25 Brown Hall, Princeton, N. J.
Occupation: Studying at Princeton Theological Seminary.

Mordecai Jackson Crispin, A. B.
Berwick, Pa.
With "The Jackson and Woodin Mfg. Co.," Berwick, Pa.

Frank Lindley Critchlow, A. B.
Mt. Hermon, Mass.
Instructor in Pingry School, Elizabeth, N. J.

Henry Haines Cross, C. E.
Mt. Holly, N. J.

Benjamin Dangerfield, Jr., A. B.
4727 Bayard St., Pittsburg, Pa.
With "The Bank of Pittsburg."

Samuel Boyer Davis, A. B.
1623 Spruce St., Philadelphia, Pa.; 11 W. H., Cambridge, Mass.
Studying at Harvard Law School.

Archibald Deming Davis, B. S.
Lakewood, N. J.
With "Samuel D. Davis & Co.," Bankers, 36 Wall St., New York.

John Ross Delafield, A. B.
475 Fifth Ave., New York; 29 Winthrop Hall, Cambridge, Mass.
Studying at Harvard Law School.

Alfred Lewis Pinneo Dennis, A. B.
301 Lexington Ave., New York.
Studying History and Political Science at Columbia University, New York.

George Goodwin Dewey, B. S.
42 Islington St., Portsmouth, N. H.
With "Joy, Langdon & Co.," Worth St., New York.

Henry Street Dickerman.*
941 South 4th St., Springfield, Ill.

William Sutton Dickson, B. S.
371 South Highland Ave., Pittsburg, Pa.; 8th St. and Duquesne Way, Pittsburg, Pa.
With "Pittsburg Department, Atlantic Refining Co."

Edward Lewis Dodd, A. B.
40 North Arlington Ave., East Orange, N. J.
Studying at College of Physicians and Surgeons, New York.

Alfred Abel Doolittle, A. B.
Temporary Address : 43 University Aall, Princeton, N. J.
Occupation : Special Fellow of Biology at Princeton University.

William Furman Doty, A. B.
1010 Massachusetts Ave., Washington, D. C. ; Gale, St. Lawrence County, N. Y.
Evangelist for two churches.

John N. Drummond, Jr.*
Occupation : With "Drummond Tobacco Co.," St, Louis, Mo.

Alexander Nelson Easton, A. B.
Summit, N. J.
On "New York Times."

David Farragut Edwards, A. B.
284 Pacific Ave., Jersey City, N. J.
Reading Law with Dickinson, Thompson & McMaster, No. 1 Exchange Place, Jersey City, N. J.

James Johnston Elliott, A. B.
Murfreesboro, Tenn. ; Lebanon, Tenn.
Studying Law at Cumberland University.

James Henry Emlen.
30 South Broad St., Trenton, N. J.

John Pinney Erdman, A. B.
Morristown, N. J.
Studying at McCormick Theological Seminary, Chicago, Ill.

Charles Milton Evans, A. B.
322 York Ave., Towanda, Pa.
With D. S. Evans, Dry Goods, 410 Main St., Towanda, Pa.

13

David Fentress, A. B.
118 Pine St., Chicago, Ill.; 29 Weld Hall, Cambridge, Mass.
Studying at Harvard Law School.

Francis Fentress, Jr.*
191 Wellington St., Memphis, Tenn.; 76 Continental Building, Memphis, Tenn.
Attorney-at-Law.

Leon Barnesconia Fish.*
Hancock, N. Y.
Teaching.

William Alexander Fisher, Jr., A. B.
905 Cathedral St., Baltimore, Md.
Studying at Johns Hopkins Medical School.

Herbert William Fitzgerald.*
525 Chestnut St., Columbia, Pa.; West Newton, Mass.
With H. H. Hunt, 166 Devonshire St., Boston, Mass.

Emory Leyden Ford, B. S.
Wyandotte, Mich.
Purchasing Agent Michigan Alkali Co., Wyandotte, Mich.

Alexander Robert Fordyce, Jr., A. B.
312 Belleville Ave., Newark, N. J.
Studying at the New York Law School.

Persifor Frazer, Jr.*
928 Spruce St., Philadelphia, Pa.
Marine Engineer. With Wm. Cramp & Sons, Ship Builders, Beach and Ball Sts., Philadelphia, Pa.

John Calvin French, Jr., A. B.
Prosperity, Pa.; 80 Alexander St., Princeton, N. J.
Studying at Princeton Theological Seminary.

Thomas Galt, Jr., A. B.
Hawarden, Ia.
Farming.

Nelson Burr Gaskill, A. B.
Mt. Holly, N. J.; 20 St. Botolph St., Boston, Mass.
Studying at Harvard Law School.

Thomas Logan Gaskill, A. B.
Mt. Holly, N. J.
Studying Law at University of Pennsylvania.

Daniel Rouse Bower Glenn.
15 Dickinson St., Princeton, N. J.
Mechanical Dentist, with Dr. J. B. Cottrell, Princeton, N. J.

Aaron William Godfrey.*
40 West 68th St., New York.
Electrical Engineer and Miner, Mexico City, Mexico.

John Randolph Graham, A. B.
Winchester, Va.; 3503a Franklin Ave., St. Louis, Mo.
Studying at Missouri Medical College, St. Louis, Mo.

Charles Henry Grant.*
Summit, N. J.
With "American Lumber Co.," 348 East 28th St., New York.

Eugene Gray, A. B.
530 Town St., Columbus, Ohio.
Business.

Louis Herbert Gray, A. B.
Princeton, N. J.
Fellow in Indo-Iranian Languages at Columbia University, New York.

Meldrum Gray, A. B.
530 Town Street, Columbus, Ohio.
Doing nothing when last heard from.

Woodward Keeling Greene, A. B.
Cedar Rapids, Ia.
With B. C. R. & N. R. R., Waterloo, Ia.

Arthur Gunster.

402 Jefferson Ave., Scranton, Pa.

Agent "Philadelphia Oil Co."

Warren Jackson Haines, A. B.

1822 Mt. Vernon St., Philadelphia, Pa.

With "J. T. Jackson & Co., Real Estate," 711 Walnut St., Philadelphia, Pa.

William Hager.

2626 Wyoming St., St. Louis, Mo.

With "C. Hager Sons & Co.," Hinge Manufacturers, St, Louis, Mo.

Louis Williams Hall, Jr.

Harrisburg, Pa.; 5518 Ellsworth Ave., Pittsburg, Pa.

With "Standard Manufacturing Co.," Allegheny, Pa.

Benjamin Schuyley Halsey, A. B.

Occupation: Manager of the "Sheffield Farms Dairy Co.," New York City, N. Y.

Edward William Hamilton, A. B.

128 Nott Terrace, Schenectady, N. Y.

Instructor at Lawrenceville School, Lawrenceville, N. J.

George Gordon Hammill, A. B.

Stamford, Conn.

Studying at New York Law School.

John Hanlon, C. E.

Occupation: With "Crown Point Mine," Briggs, Arizona.

Norris William Harkness, Jr., A. B.

916 Clinton St., Philadelphia, Pa.; 20 Brown Hall, Princeton, N.J.

Studying at Princeton Theological Seminary.

William Prettyman Hearn.

1120 Walnut St., Philadelphia, Pa.

Studying at Jefferson Medical College, Philadelphia, Pa.

Sharon P. Heilman.*

Kittanning, Pa.; 3705 Woodland Ave., Philadelphia, Pa.

Studying Medicine at University of Pennsylvania.

David Boynton Helm.*
Occupation: Charge of Estates, 95 Nassau St., Room 103, New York.

David Ford Henry.*
141 North Avenue. Allegheny, Pa.
Manager "The Pittsburg Terra-Cotta Co.," Pittsburg, Pa.

Christian Stanger Heritage, C. E.
Glassboro, N. J.; 1004 King St., Wilmington, Del.
Civil Engineer, P. W. and B. R. R.

Charles Avery Hickey, A. B.
78 Front St., Binghamton, N. Y.
Studying Law.

Edward Blachard Hodge, Jr., A. B.
319 South 41st St., Philadelphia, Pa.
Studying Medicine at the University of Pennsylvania.

Frederick Evans Hoffman, A. B.
200 West Berry St., Fort Wayne, Ind.
With "Hoffman Bros.," Fort Wayne, Ind.

Edward Wilson Holmes.*
235 South Hill St., Los Angeles, Cal.
Representing "Penn Mutual Life Insurance Co. of Philadelphia,"
    320 Byrne Building, Los Angeles, Cal.

Isaac Smith Homans.*
Englewood, N. J.
With "The Spectator Co.," 95 William St., New York.

Alfred Muirhead Howell, A. B.
Cogan Station, Pa.
Secretary and Treasurer Times Publishing Co., Williamsport, Pa.

Daniel James Hoyt.*
40 Dewitt St., Amsterdam, N. Y.; 404 Union St., Schenectady, N. Y.
Studying at Union College, Class of '99.

Charles Ridgely Hudson.*
Springfield, Ill.
With "Ridgely National Bank," Springfield, Ill.

Augustine Leftwich Humes, A. B.
Knoxville, Tenn.; 1 Felton Hall, Cambridge, Mass.
Studying at Harvard Law School.

Alexander Jackson, A. B.
98 South Franklin St., Wilkes-Barre, Pa.
Reading Law in Office of Hon. D. L. Rhone, 7 South Franklin St.,
Wilkes-Barre, Pa.

William Herron Jamison, A. B.
67 Union Ave., Allegheny, Pa.
Studying at Allegheny Theological Seminary.

Archibald Todd Johnson, A. B.
833 North 22d St., Philadelphia, Pa.

Clarence Melville Johnson, A. B.
1316 Vermont Ave., Washington, D. C.
Studying at the Columbian University Law School.

Gordon Johnston, A. B.
1721 Twelfth Ave. South, Birmingham, Ala.; Memphis, Tenn.
With "Buck-Johnston Abstract Co.," Memphis, Tenn.

Alfred Bloomfield Jones.
Mt. Holly, N. J.; 1915 Fifth Ave., Pittsburg, Pa.
Civil Engineer, P. C. C. & St. L. R. R. Co.

Jesse Dilley Jones.
143 Franklin St., Wilkes-Barre, Pa.; Care Evening Leader, Car-
bondale, Pa.
Journalist.

Thomas Mifflin Jones, Jr.*
15 Stockton Ave., Allegheny, Pa.
With "Jones & Laughlins Co., Ltd.," Steel Manufacturers, Pittsburg, Pa.

Percy Ogden Judson, B. S.
Kingston, N. Y.
With "Herbert Brush Manufacturing Co.," Kingston, N. Y.

John Campbell Kerr, A. B.
Englewood, N. J.
Studying at Columbia Law School, New York.

Carlton Montgomery Kershow, B. S.
2019 Spruce St., Philadelphia.
Gentleman of leisure.

Alfred Gedney Killmer, A. B.
120 Crescent Ave., Plainfield, N. J.; 701 Drexel Building, Philadelphia, Pa.
Studying at University of Pennsylvania Law School.

John Douglas Kilpatrick, C. E.
1027 St. Paul St., Baltimore, Md.; Colonial Club, Princeton, N. J.
Studying Electrical Engineering at Princeton University.

Kenneth Raleigh Kingsbury.
63 Evergreen Place, East Orange, N. J.; Lancaster, Pa.
With Standard Oil Co.

Francis Marschalk Kip.
Harlingen, N. J.

LeRoy Gresham Kirkman, A. B.
17 Sussex St., Port Jervis, N. Y.
Studying at College of Physicians and Surgeons, New York City.

Bernard Stallo Kittredge.*
Avondale, Cincinnati, Ohio.
With Kittredge & Wilby, Attorneys-at-Law, 604–7 Neave Building, Cincinnati, Ohio.

James Carnahan Knight, A. B.
442 Belden Ave., Chicago, Ill.

Robert Ryland Knight, A. B.
Shelbyville, Ky.; Baptist Seminary, Louisville, Ky.
Studying at the Southern Baptist Theological Seminary, Louisville, Ky.

Edwin Edward Kurtzeborn, B. S.
3626 West Pine Boulevard, St. Louis, Mo.
Studying at Marion Sims College of Medicine, St. Louis, Mo.

William Edward Lampe, A. B.
206 North Market St., Frederick, Md.; 302 Hodge Hall, Princeton, N. J.
Studying at Princeton Theological Seminary.

Langdon Lea.
Care J. T. Lea & Co., Stephen Girard Building, Philadelphia, Pa.
With "Cannelton Coal Co.," Cannelton, Kanawha Co., W. Va.

Frederick Curwen Leas, B. S.
400 South 40th St., Philadelphia, Pa.
With Leas & McVitty, Leather, 301 North 3d St., Philadelphia, Pa.

LeRoy Porter Leas, A. B.
400 South 40th St., Philadelphia, Pa.
With Leas & McVitty, Leather, 40 South St., Boston, Mass.

Thomas Dimock Leonard.
710 Lodi St., Syracuse, N. Y.
Doing nothing when last heard from.

William Wirt Leonard, A. B.
Salisbury, Md.
Studying Law at the University of Virginia, Charlottesville, Va.

Welding Dennis Libbey, B. S.
Temporary Address: Care of F. A. Libbey, 45 Broadway, New
York City.

Robert Lincoln Litch, A. B.
115 Center St., Bethlehem, Pa.
Teaching in Harry Hillman Academy, Bethlehem, Pa.

Robert Forsyth Little, Jr., A. B.
116 West 76th St., New York City; 63 Wall St., New York City.
Studying at New York Law School.

Frederick William Loetscher, A. B.
1015 Lincoln Ave., Dubuque, Ia.; Princeton, N. J.
Studying at Princeton Theological Seminary.

Joseph Mackey Roseberry Long, A. B.
55 West 121st St., New York City; 111 Broadway, care Otis &
Pressinger, New York City.
Studying at New York Law School.

John Hancock Louser, A. B.
114 South 9th St., Lebanon, Pa.
Reading Law in Office of ex-Judge F. E. Weily, 25 North 9th St.,
Lebanon, Pa.

Albert Howe Lybyer, A. B.
Brazil, Ind.; Princeton, N. J.
Studying at Princeton Theological Seminary.

William Thomas Lyle, C. E.
203 South 6th St., Newark, N. J.
Assistant Engineer with Essex County Park Commission.

George Wood Lyon, B. S.
Bridgeton, N. J.; Box 177, Cape Town, South Africa (via England.)
With " H. W. Peabody & Co." (52 New St., New York), Importers,
Cape Town, South Africa.

David André L'Esperance, Jr.*
2060 Madison Ave., New York.
Practising Law with " E. L. Fanshaw and W. H. Harris," 229
Broadway, New York.

Charles Lawrence Martin.*
Summit, N. J.
With Petrolia Mfg. Co., Soaps, 24 Grove St., New York City.

Charles Ingalls Marvin, B. S.
Germantown, Pa.; Tarrytown, N. Y.
With N. Y. C. and H. R. R. Co., Comptroller's Office, New York City.

Benjamin Allen Mason, Jr., A. B.
Albia, Ia.; Princeton, N. J.
Studying at Princeton Theological Seminary.

William Arnot Mather, A. B.
16 West 122d St., New York City, Hosmer Hall, Hartford, Conn.
Studying at Hartford Theological Seminary.

William Francis Mattingly, Jr., A. B.
1616 H St., N. W., Washington, D. C.; 435 7th St., N. W., Washington, D. C.
Studying at Columbian University Law School.

Samuel Hewes Mattson.*
Sharon Hill, Pa.
With Pennsylvania Heat, Light & Power Co., 10th and Sansome
streets, Philadelphia, Pa.

Robert Maxwell.
East Greenwich, N. Y.; 133 North Ave., Allegheny, Pa.
Studying at Allegheny Theological Seminary.

Laurence Johnson Mead.*
100 East 39th St., New York City.
With R. Hoe & Co., Printing Presses, 504 Grand St., New York City.

Albert Goodsell Milbank, A. B.
42 West 38th St., New York City.
Studying at New York Law School.

Dennis Long Miller.*
1326 4th Ave., Louisville, Ky.
Secretary "Dennis Long & Co.," Louisville, Ky.; Treasurer "Owensboro Water Co.," Owensboro, Ky.

Joseph Walter Miller, A. B.
Friesburg, N. J.
Studying at Auburn Theological Seminary, Auburn, N. Y.

Samuel Wilson Miller, Jr., A. B.
Saltsburg, Pa.; 202 West 78th St., New York City.
Studying at New York Law School.

Edward Kirkpatrick Mills, A. B.
66 Macculloch Ave., Morristown, N. J.; 238 West 132d St., New York City.
Studying at Columbia Law School.

Frederic Livingstone Mills, A. B.
550 Fulton street, Jamaica, N. Y.
With "Metropolitan Street Railway Co.," Law Department, 621 Broadway, New York City.

William Galbraith Mitchell, C. E.
1522 31st St., Washington, D. C.
With "General Electric Co.," Schenectady, N. Y. Students' Course.

George Franklin Moll, A. B.
Highland, Kan.
Farming.

John James Moment, A. B.
Orono, Ontario; 203 Hodge Hall, Princeton, N. J.
Studying at Princeton Theological Seminary.

Harry Morgan Moore, A. B.
California, Mo.; 3224 Washington Ave., St. Louis, Mo.
Studying at St. Louis Medical College.

Minot Canfield Morgan, A. B.
Remsenburg, N. Y.
At present traveling in the Orient. Expects to return to Princeton
Theological Seminary next year.

Roland Sletor Morris, A. B.
Knox and Coulter Aves., Germantown, Pa.
Studying Law at the University of Pennsylvania, and in office of
J. de F. Junkin, 6th and Walnut Sts., Philadelphia.

Frederick Pooley Mudge, A. B.
44 Mercer St., Princeton, N. J.; 409 Hodge Hall, Princeton, N. J.
Studying in Princeton Theological Seminary.

William Henry Musser, A. B.
215 North Second St., Harrisburg, Pa.
Teaching in Harrisburg High School.

Joseph Lawrence Myers, A. B.
517 East Front St., Plainfield, N. J.; care Handy & Harmon, 32
Nassau St., New York City.
With Handy & Harmon, Bankers, 32 Nassau St., New York City.

Francis Charles McDonald, A. B.
Temporary Address: Worthington, Armstrong Co., Pa.
Occupation: Private Tutor.

Robert McNutt McElroy, A. B.
Lexington, Ky.; University Athletic Club, New York City.
Private Tutor.

John Capell McFarlan.*
64 Church St., Amsterdam, N. Y.
With McFarlan & Co., Knit Goods Manufacturers, Amsterdam,
N. Y.

Richard Philip McGraun.
"Grand View," Lancaster, Pa.
Stock Farming.

Wilbur Clyde McGregor.*
Wheeling, W. Va.

William Strong McGuire, A. B.
315 West 75th St., New York City.
Studying at New York Law School.

Scott McLanahan, A. B.
Chambersburg, Pa.; 318 West 57th St., New York City.
Studying at New York Law School.

Wallace Donald McLean, A. B.`
1414 Park St., N. W., Washington, D. C.
Studying at Columbia University Law School.

John Evans McLain.*
401 Park Ave., Johnstown, Pa.
With "The Johnson Co.," Johnstown, Pa.

Charles Bell McMullen, A. B.
Tarkio, Mo.; Princeton, N. J.
Studying at Princeton Theological Seminary.

John Hobart McMurdy.*
P. O. Box 760, Salt Lake City, Utah.
With Taylor & Bounton Ore Sampling Co., Salt Lake City, Utah.

Clarence Egberts Newman.*
258 State St., Albany, N. Y.
With Mechanics & Farmers Bank, Albany, N. Y.

Harold Byron Northrup, B. S.
Johnstown, N. Y.
With "Northrup Glove Manufacturing Co.," Johnstown, N. Y.

William Vastine Oglesby, A. B.
Danville, Pa.

Frank Clifford Okey, A. B.
Corning, Ia.
With Corning State Savings Bank, Corning, Ia.

Willette Bronson Orr, A. B.
Chambersburg, Pa.
With "Valley National Bank," and also reading law with firm o
Sharpe & Sharpe, Chambersburg, Pa.

Samuel Roosevelt Outerbridge, (C. E., Harvard.)*
252 West 78th St., New York City; 145 Washington St., Buffalo,
N. Y., care Buffalo Terminal Railway.
Civil Engineer on N. Y. C. and H. R. R. Co.

Singleton Peabody Outhwaite, A. B.
289 East State St., Columbus, Ohio.
Studying at New York Law School.

John Rosseel Overton, A. B.
305 York Ave., Towanda, Pa.

David Park, A. B.
Corinth, Miss.; McCormick Seminary, Chicago, Ill.
Studying at McCormick Theological Seminary, Chicago, Ill.

Frederick Dalton Parker, B. S.
203 McDougal St., Fostoria, Ohio; 111 East 45th St., New York
City.
Studying at New York Law School, and with law firm of Ulman &
Parker, 120 Broadway, New York City.

William Bowne Parsons, B. S.
Flushing, N. Y.; 51 Liberty St., New York City.
With "H. H. Cammann & Co."

Charles Edgar Patton, A. B.
Warrior's Mark, Pa.; 52 Brown Hall, Seminary, Princeton, N. J.
Studying at Princeton Theological Seminary.

Robert Hunter Patton, II., A. B.
"Prospect," Princeton, N. J.
Studying at New York Law School.

Frederick Marshall Paul, A. B.

3 Madison Ave., Newark, N. J.; 1126 Spruce St., Philadelphia, Pa.
Studying Medicine at the University of Pennsylvania.

Albert Irving Payne, C. E.

Sayville, N. Y.; 19 Arlington St., Westminster, S. W., London,
England.
With "Economical Gas Apparatus Constructing Co."

Ralph Barton Perry, A. B.

54 West 55th St., New York City; 1689 Cambridge St., Cambridge,
Mass.
Taking Post-Graduate Course in Philosophy at Harvard.

Arthur Edmund Pew, B. S.

715 North Hiland Ave., Pittsburg, Pa.; 248 4th Ave., Pittsburg, Pa.
General Purchasing Agent, "The Sun Oil Co."

Gaston Pearson Philip.*

1230 Connecticut Ave., Washington, D. C.

Harry Gordon Pierce, A. B.

Temporary Address: 23 West 76th St., New York City.
Occupation: Private Tutor. Also studying at New York Law
School.

Talbot Eugene Pierce, A. B.

Waterford, Loudoun County, Va.; Hazleton, Pa.
With A. S. Van Wickle, Hazleton, Pa.

Micajah Wallace Pope.

Annapolis, Md.; 36 Wall St., New York City; 60 West 58th St.,
New York City.

John Albert Potter, A. B.

Franklin, Delaware Co., N. Y.; Tarrytown, N. Y.
Teaching Latin and English at Irving Institute, Tarrytown, N. Y.

David Potter, A. B.

143 Broad St., Bridgeton, N. J.; Care of Navy Department, Washington, D. C.
Assistant Paymaster United States Navy.

William Woodburn Potter, B. S.
1913 Spruce St., Philadelphia, Pa.; 320 Walnut St., Philadelphia, Pa.
With Cope & Stewardson, Architects, Philadelphia, Pa.

Edgar Fitz Randolph, II.*
116 South St., Morristown, N. J.
With "Building and Sanitary Inspection Co.," 55 Liberty St., New York City.

Oliver W. Rafferty.*
614-5 Lewis Block, Pittsburg, Pa.; 306 South 13th St., Philadelphia, Pa.
Agent for Empire Portland Cement Co.

William Belden Reed, Jr., C. E.
162 West 121st St., New York City.
Civil Engineer, Metropolitan Street Railway Co.

Stanley Chester Reese, A. B., A. M.
633 Summerlea St., E. E., Pittsburg, Pa.; 6 S. M. R., Princeton, N. J.
Thaw University Fellow in Astronomy, Princeton University.

Thomas Ridgway.*
1706 Locust St., Philadelphia, Pa.
With "Real Estate Investment Co.," 721 Walnut St., Philadelphia, Pa.

Joseph Cottrell Righter, Jr., A. B.
15 Trinity Place, Williamsport, Pa.; Care of "Daily Sun," Williamsport, Pa.
With "Williamsport Daily Sun."

Samuel Gayle Riley, A. B.
Greenville, S. C.; 506 East Liberty St., Ann Arbor, Mich.
Studying Law at University of Michigan.

George Barclay Rives, A. B.
152 Madison Ave., New York City; Care of Manhattan Trust Co., 20 Wall St., New York City.
With "Manhattan Trust Co.," New York City.

Algernon Brooke Roberts, B. S.
Bala, Pa.
Studying Law at University of Pennsylvania.

Robert Sinclaire Rodgers, B. S.
92 North Limestone St., Springfield, Ohio.

Henry Welsh Rogers, B. S.
Chestnut Hill, Philadelphia, Pa.; Chestnut and Water Sts., Philadelphia, Pa.
With Rogers, Holloway & Co., Exporters and Importers, Philadelphia, Pa.

Joseph George Rosengarten, Jr., A. B.
325 South 11th St., Philadelphia, Pa.; Station D, Philadelphia, Pa.
With "Rosengarten & Sons," Manufacturing Chemists, Philadelphia, Pa.

Frederick Tupper Saussy, A. B.
143 Gordon St., Savannah, Ga.
Superintendent of Savannah Board of Trade.

Anselm Edwin Schaff.*
Merrick, L. I., N. Y.

John Hinsdale Scheide, A. B.
Titusville, Pa.; Woodville, Sandusky Co., Ohio.
With "Ohio Oil Co."

William Henry Schoonmaker.
4940 Ellsworth Ave., Pittsburg, Pa.
Gentleman of Leisure.

Edward Lyman Sheldon.*
Care E. W. Sheldon, 45 Wall St., New York City.
With "Walden & Benham," Importers and Exporters, 101 Water St., New York City.

John Charles Sherriff, A. B.
59 Union Ave., Allegheny, Pa.
With "Sherriff Machinery Co.," Pittsburg, Pa., and Studying at the Pittsburg Law School.

William Duncan Silkworth, A. B.
Fishkill, N. Y.

Studying at College of Physicians and Surgeons.

George Rosengarten Sinnickson, C. E.
230 West Rittenhouse Square, Philadelphia, Pa.; Care A. L.
Stout, Room 379 Broad St. Station, P. R. R., Philadelphia, Pa.

Civil Engineer on Pennsylvania Railroad.

James Dunn Small, A. B.
"The Vincennes," 3601 Vincennes Ave., Chicago, Ill.

Studying Law at Chicago College of Law (Lake Forest), and at
office of Jos. D. Morris, 1317 Chamber of Commerce, Chicago,
Ill.

Lloyd Llewellyn Smith, C. E.
906 Carteret Ave., Trenton, N. J.; University of Leipzig, Germany.

Studying at University of Leipzig.

Ralph Brown Smith, A. B.
Blairsville, Pa.

With New York Branch of "Garden City Wire and Spring Co., of
Chicago," 436 Canal St., New York City.

Ralph Dusenbury Smith, B. S.
131 Front St., Binghamton, N. Y.; "The Judson," Washington
Square, South, New York City.

Studying at New York Law School.

Thomas Cummings Smith, Jr.*
325 South 5th St., Springfield, Ill.

William Wessendrew Smith.*
325 South 5th St., Springfield, Ill.

Francis Sydney Smithers, Jr., A. B.
507 Madison Ave., New York City; 175 Ninth Ave., New York
City.

Studying at the General Theological Seminary, New York City.

Homer Clay Snitcher, A. B.

Greenwich, N. J.

Studying at Princeton Theological Seminary.

William Francis Mattingly Sowers, A. B.

1320 New York Ave., Washington, D. C.; 515 Cathedral St., Baltimore, Md.

Studying at Johns Hopkins Medical School.

Oliver Bennett Sprecher.*

141 South 8th St., Reading, Pa.

Samuel Robert Spriggs, A. B.

Livingston Manor, New York; 56 Brown Hall, Seminary, Princeton, N. J.

Studying at Princeton Theological Seminary.

Charles Anthony Stein.*

159 West 64th St., New York City.

With "Standard Varnish Works," 29 Broadway, New York City.

Francis Gray Stewart, C. E.

27 East 38th St., New York City.

Studying at Columbia College; also in office of C. L. W. Eidlitz, 160 Fifth Ave., New York.

Thomas Henry Atherton Stites, A. B.

Wyoming, Pa.; 380 Ludlow St., Philadelphia, Pa.

Studying Medicine at University of Pennsylvania.

William LeRoy Stockton, A. B.

98 Mercer St., Princeton, N. J.; 20 East Jersey St.; Elizabeth, N. J.

With Prudential Insurance Co., Room 816, Prudential Building, Newark. N. J.

Joseph Herbert Stopp, A. B.

34 North 5th St., Allentown, Pa.; Care Biddle & Ward, 505 Chestnut St., Philadelphia, Pa.

Studying Law in offices of Biddle & Ward.

Archibald Alexander Talmage.*
Belmar, N. J.; 120 Broadway, New York City.
Representing Equitable Life Assurance Society.

William Paton Thomson, A. B.
1217 Eighth Ave., Altoona, Pa.
Manager and General Agent for "Maintenance of Way Improvement Co.," Altoona, Pa.

Paul Tillinghast, A. B.
Englewood, N. J.; 173 Broadway, New York City.
With "Provident Savings Life Assurance Society."

Walter Clark Titus.
495 West State St., Trenton, N. J.
With "Philadelphia Oil Co.," 106 North Water St., Philadelphia, Pa.

Warren Merwin Tower, A. B.
340 Clinton St., Brooklyn, N. Y.
With "Tower & Lyon," Hardware, 95 Chambers St., New York City.

John Moore Trout, A. B.
Bridgeville, Del.
Studying at Hartford Theological Seminary, Hartford, Conn.

Charles Dunbar Trumbull.
521 Wabash Ave., Kansas City, Mo.; 1426 St. Louis Ave., Kansas City, Mo.
With "Trumbull Seed Co.," Kansas City, Mo.

Edward Bates Turner, A. B.
Corning, Ia.
Studying at Auburn Theological Seminary.

Horatio Whitridge Turnbull.
1629 Park Ave., Baltimore, Md.; 219 West 23d St., New York City.
With "American Telegraph and Telephone Co.," 16 Dey St., New York.

Ralph Ernest Urban, A. B.

Woodbury, N. J.; Chelsea Square, New York.
Studying at General Theological Seminary, New York.

Herbert Ure, A. B.

340 Thirteenth Ave., Newark, N. J.; 404 Hodge Hall, Princeton, N. J.
Studying at Princeton Theological Seminary.

George Dawes Van Arsdale, B. S.

175 Orchard St., Newark, N. J.; 71 Beaulieu St., Detroit.
Chemist, with "Parke Davis & Co.," Detroit, Mich.

Frank Phineas Van Syckel, A. B.

Princeton, N. J.
Teaching.

William Wiswell Verner.*

167 Western Ave., Allegheny, Pa.; Hahnemann Medical College, North Broad St., Philadelphia, Pa.
Studying Medicine at Hahnemann Medical College, Philadelphia, Pa.

Montgomery Blair Wailes.*

Leonardtown, Md.; Spencer's Wharf, Md.
Practising Law.

Harry Godfrey Waring.*

Yonkers, N. Y.
With "Provident Savings Life Assurance Society," New York City.

Edwards Pierrepont Ward, A. B.

Dansville, N. Y.
Reading Law in office of Rowe & Fairchild, Dansville, N. Y.

Frank Hawley Ward, A. B.

12 Grove Place, Rochester, N. Y.; 6 S. E. B., Princeton, N. J.
Studying Electrical Engineering at Princeton University.

Dorr Eugene Warner, A. B.
Unionville, Ohio; 51 Andale St., Cleveland, Ohio.
Studying Law at Western Reserve Law School, Cleveland, Ohio.

John Waterhouse, A. B.
Honolulu, Hawaiian Islands.
With J. T. Waterhouse, Importer, Honolulu.

George Henry Waters, A. B.
Peekskill, N. Y.; Trevor Hall, Rochester, N. Y.
Studying at Rochester Theological Seminary.

Leon Joseph Wayave, Jr., A. B.
129 East 2d St., Corning, N. Y.

Paul Charles Weed, A. B.
261 Summit Ave., St. Paul, Minn.; German-American Bank Building, St. Paul, Minn.
Special Agent, Phœnix Insurance Co.

Arthur Ledlie Wheeler, B. S.
400 Chestnut St., Philadelphia, Pa.

Charles Hallock Whitehead, B. S.
3912 Troost Ave., Kansas City, Mo.
Real Estate, 801 Wyandotte St., Kansas City, Mo.

Thomas Young Wickham, Jr., A. B.
Ainsworth, Iowa.
Studying at Harvard Law School.

Charles Gordon Wiestling.
Vandalia, Ill.

Charles Frederick Williams, A. B.
300 Lexingon Ave., New York City.
Studying at Harvard Law School.

Curtis Moore Willock, A. B.
153 North Ave., Allegheny, Pa.; 10 Frisbie Place, Cambridge, Mass.
Studying at Harvard Law School.

Charles Alexander Wilson, A. B.
Tarkio, Mo.; Stuttgart, Ark.
Professor of German and History, Stuttgart College, Arkansas.

William Rolla Wilson, A. B.
1273 Corona St., Denver, Col.

Arthur Edward Winter, B. S.
25 Berkeley Ave., Orange, N. J.
With Winter & Smillie, Bankers, 62 Wall St., New York City.

Charles Wesyler Wisner, Jr., A. B.
2435 St. Paul St., Baltimore, Md.; Beirut, Syria.
Instructor in American Protestant College, Beirut, Syria.

George Watson Womack, Jr.*
354 Bates Ave., St Paul, Minn.; Broadway and 3d St., St. Paul, Minn.
With Farwell, Ozmun, Kirk & Co., Wholesale Hardware, St. Paul, Minn.

Charles Ladd Woodburn, A. B.
21 Main St., Towanda, Pa.
Studying at University of Pennsylvania Medical School.

Edward Strong Worcester, A. B.
15 Elmwood Ave., Burlington, Vt.; 14 N. D., Princeton, N. J.
Instructor in Latin, Princeton University.

Willard Jurey Wright, A. B.
Lebanon, Ohio.
Deputy Probate Judge, Warren Co., Ohio.

Philip Walter Yarrow, A. B.
7 Congress St., Lowell, Mass.
Studying at Hartford Theological Seminary, Hartford, Conn.

Jesse Reinhart Zeigler, A. B.
Mercer, Mercer Co., Pa.; 1 Brown Hall, Seminary, Princeton, N. J.
Studying at Princeton Theological Seminary.

Recapitulation.

Business	93
Law	56
Theology	35
Occupations Unknown	26
Medicine	22
Teaching	16
Engineering	8
Studying	8
Journalism	5
Gentlemen of Leisure	5
Electricity	4
Farming	3
Practising Law	3
Architecture	2
United States Navy	1
Preaching	1
Traveling	1
Total active membership	289

Members at Graduation	232
Active ex-members	57
Inactive ex-members	42
Total membership	331

In Memory

of our classmate,

Harry Beam Campbell,

who died at Chicago, Illinois,

October 16, 1897.

In Memory

of our classmate,

Sydney Serrill Bunting,

who died at his home,

No. 2114 Spruce St., Philadelphia, Pa.,

February 20, 1897.

Where Ninety Six is Living.

❧

THE appended lists of members of the class, arranged according to their places of temporary or permanent residence, have been compiled in the hope that they may at some time be useful to members of the class, to our Alumni Associations or to any Princetonian who may desire to reach the Ninety Six men living in or near some of our largest cities.

These lists are intended to include the names of all Ninety Six men who live within a radius of thirty miles of the several cities. The addresses may be ascertained by reference to the roll of membership foregoing. When a man resides in one of the cities mentioned, and is temporarily located near another, his name appears under both heads. Which is the permanent and which the temporary address can be determined by consulting the membership roll.

New York.—Alford, G. K. Allen, Atkinson, Baylis, Bergen, Bishop, Blackmore, Bostwick, Bower, Briggs, Brockway, O. I. Brown, H. Bruen, J. Bruen, Byington, Chandler, Clark, Cochran, Coe, T. Conover, Critchlow, A. D. Davis, Delafield, Dennis, Dewey, Dodd, Easton, Edwards, Fordyce, Grant, L. H. Gray, Halsey, Hammill, Helm, Homans, Kerr, Kingsbury, Kirkman, Libbey, Little, Long, Lyle, L'Esperance, Martin, Marvin, McGuire, McLanahan, Mather, Mead, Milbank, S. W. Miller, E. K. Mills, F. L. Mills, Myers, McElroy, S. Outerbridge, Outhwaite Parker, Parsons, Paul, Perry, H. G. Pierce, Pope, J. A. Potter, Randolph, Reed, Rives, Schaff, Sheldon, Silkworth, R. B. Smith, R. D. Smith, Smithers, Stein, Stewart, Stockton, Talmage, Tillinghast, Tower, Turnbull, Urban, Ure, Van Arsdale, Waring, C. F. Williams, Winter.

Total... **86**

Philadelphia.—F. O. Allen, Bloch, Bowman, Brace, Bronson, Brooks, C. Browne, Bush, Cadwalader, Carnochan, Churchman, Corser, Cross, S. B. Davis, Frazer, N. B. Gaskill, T. L. Gaskill, Haines, Harkness, Hearn, Heilman, Heritage, Hodge, A. T. Johnson, A. B. Jones, Kershow, Killmer, Lea, F. C. Leas, L. P. Leas, Mattson, Morris, Paul, W. W. Potter, Ridgway, Roberts, Rogers, Rosengarten, Sinnickson, Stites, Stopp, Titus, Verner, Wheeler, Woodburn.

 Total 45

Princeton.—Beam, Blackwell, Bloch, Brearley, Briggs, Bronson, A. H. Brown, Crawford, Doolittle, French, Glenn, L. H. Gray, Hamilton, Harkness, Kilpatrick, Lampe, Loetscher, Lybyer, McMullen, Mason, Moment, Mudge, Patton, Reese, Snitcher, Spriggs, Stockton, Van Syckel, F. H. Ward, Worcester, Zeigler.

 Total 32

Pittsburg.—Bower, Dangerfield, Dickson, L. W. Hall, Henry, Jamison, A. B. Jones, T. M. Jones, Maxwell, Pew, Rafferty, Reese, Schoonmaker, Sherriff, Verner, Willock.

 Total 16

Boston.—Bissell, S. B. Davis, Delafield, D. Fentress, Fitzgerald, N. B. Gaskill, Humes, L. P. Leas, Perry, Wickham, C. F. Williams, Willock.

 Total 12

Baltimore.—Fisher, Kilpatrick, W. W. Leonard, Pope, Sowers, Turnbull, Wailes.

 Total 7

Washington.—Armes, C. M. Johnson, McLean, Mattingly, Philip, D. Potter, Sowers.

 Total 7

St. Louis.—H. C. Adams, Drummond, Graham, Hager, Kurtzeborn, Moore.

 Total 6

Chicago.—Chamberlain, Erdman, D. Fentress, J. C. Knight, Park, Small.

 Total 6

To the Ex-Members of the Class.

ﾟ✦

AT the very beginning of his work every class secretary is confronted with a difficult problem, namely, whether every one who has been a member of the class, no matter for how brief a period, shall be enrolled on the list of membership. Of those men who leave college before the end of their course, there are some who, though their stay at Princeton may have been limited to a few months, give constant evidence of a loyalty to the Alma Mater unsurpassed even by the men who were fortunate enough to complete their four years' stay; others become members of sister colleges, and find their affiliations there; but there are still others who preserve a silence that tends to make the class forget them as they seem to have forgotten us. Our class is no exception to the rule, for the number of those who "fell by the wayside" is legion.

The fairest way seems to be to let the ex-members prove their interest or indifference; and this is the course your secretary has tried to follow. During the year after graduation, the ex-members received from the class secretary the same attention as the graduates of the class, and then in May last this letter was sent to those ex-members who made no response to the several class letters of the year 1896–7:

"MAY 24, 1897.

" During the past year I have been sending you, as a regular member of the Class of Ninety Six of Princeton, all the official letters and circulars issued by me as class secretary. Although your connection with the class did not extend throughout the regular four-years' course, I have, during the past year, considered you a regular member of the class. I have sent you letters that required the courtesy of an answer, leaving aside the consideration of devotion to the college. You have so far failed to reply to any of my letters.

" The unpleasant conclusion is being forced upon me that your interest in the class and in Princeton has decreased, and that you no longer desire to interest yourself in the welfare of your fellow classmates of Ninety Six. Your own persistent silence and failure to respond to my letters has led me to accept this conclusion. I trust that you will realize that the duties of the secretary of a class of 350 members are not slight, and that these duties are considerably increased by the failure of some members to reply to letters. Therefore, unless you answer this letter, I shall be obliged to make it my last communication with you on class matters.

"If I do not hear from you on or before July 1st, in response, I will accept your silence as a determination to no longer identify yourself with the class, and will drop your name from the rolls, and will send you no class letters in future.

"I wish to assure you of my desire to serve you in all matters pertaining to our class, and sincerely hope you will let me hear from you.

"Awaiting your reply, I am, yours for Ninety Six,

C. B. BOSTWICK,
Class Secretary."

In sending this letter, it was not the desire of your secretary to deal arbitrarily with the men who had not answered the class letters, but rather his wish to be able to devote his time and services only to those men who evince their desire to be active, loyal members of the class.

Therefore, on July 1st, 1897, the names of the men on the appended list were dropped from the rolls, as no letters had come from them, although prompt response was made by many to whom the above letter was sent, who had previously been remiss in their correspondence. If any of the men whose names are given below wish to be reinstated upon the class rolls, and will write to the secretary, it will be both his pleasure and his duty to comply with their request.

LIST OF EX-MEMBERS DROPPED FROM THE ROLLS.

S. H. M. Agens, L. F. Appleman, J. Auchincloss, D. W. Bates, W. H. Bean, R. Bedle, R. Billings, C. D. Burt, J. K. Cain, H. F. Chamberlain, E. E. Conover, G. J. Drew, E. G. Faile, I. L. Fiscus, R. H. Greene, F. M. Hall, H. M. Harriman, J. B. Hatfield, C. C. Henshaw, C. R. Hudson, W. L. Johnson, I. G. Koka, L. D. La Monte, P. Loving, J. J. Moffitt, A. Neyhart, E. B. Ogden, F. R. Outerbridge, O. Petty, J. P. Poe, Jr., A. Roesler, Jr., C. Roland, W. M. Sterry, G. Taggart, B. H. Warner, Jr., L. A. White, R. M. Wilkins, R. F. Williams, H. B. Wilson, M. Winton, J. L. Woldenberg, G. R. Work—42 members.

Matters Financial.

❧

T has been a cause of great regret to the class secretary, and undoubtedly no unqualified delight to the class, that almost every class letter has had to touch on the question of the class funds, and, more than that, has had to ask the members for assessments for varying amounts. Class finances are hard enough to direct when the men are in college, but when the class is scattered the difficulties are multiplied. So often has necessary mention been made of the depleted state of the class treasury, that it has seemed best to include in the present book the account of receipts and expenses given in the annexed report.

It will be seen that, to supply a present deficiency of funds, it has been necessary to borrow from the Decennial Memorial Fund the sum of $149.25, which loan is covered by unpaid Class-Day and Sesquicentennial assessments amounting to $164. But it is manifestly unfair that money subscribed by *a part of the class* for a specific purpose should be used to cover a deficit in the *general* fund, caused by the failure of some members to meet their obligations; and it will be the persistent endeavor of the secretary to see that this temporary loan is repaid at the earliest possible moment. Of course this can not be more easily effected than by prompt action on the part of members in arrears in settling their accounts.

The class has at present no outstanding obligations beside this loan from the Decennial Fund, and the expenses of publication of this "Class Record," which latter will be amply provided for by the cash on hand and the receipt of subscriptions for the book, subsequent to its publication. Every man who has not yet subscribed for a copy of the book is requested to do so as soon as possible and thus assist in the reduction of the class liabilities.

Amount handed to the Class Secretary by the Class-Day Committee.............	$133.77
Receipts from sale of tickets to the Class Supper, June 10, 1896.................	388.50
Class Day dues paid since graduation......	40.00
Assessments for Reunion, June, 1897......	35.50
Sundry·receipts...........................	11.61
Class pins sold.....	4.50
Sesquicentennial assessments paid........	608.04
"Class Records" paid for in advance to date	88.97
	$1,310.89
Amount temporarily loaned to Class from Memorial Fund......................	149.25—$1,460.14

EXPENSES.

Expenses for Class Supper, June 10, 1896...	$463.69
Expenses for Sesquicentennial Reunion....	718.21
Expenses for Reunion, June, 1897.........	55.94
Expenses for Reunion, October 30, 1897....	10.85
Postage, Printing and Stationery..........	105.07
Sundry Expenses..........................	9.19
Interest on loan from Memorial Fund......	2.95
Expenses to date for publication of "Class Record".............................	23.65
	$1,389.55
Cash on hand March 4, 1898...............	70.59—$1,460.14

RESOURCES.

Sesquicentennial assessments unpaid......	$111.00
Class Day assessments unpaid............	53.00
Cash on hand, March 4, 1898..............	70.59— $234.59

LIABILITIES.

Due to Decennial Fund for loan...........	$149.25
Approximate additional cost of publication of the "Class Record"................	80.00
	$229.25
Balance	5.34— $234.59

Respectfully submitted,

C. B. BOSTWICK, *Secretary and Treasurer.*

The Decennial Memorial Fund.

❧

AMONG previous classes it has generally been the custom to raise the fund for the "Memorial" presented to the University at the Decennial Reunion of the Class, by calling for subscriptions from the members a short while before that reunion takes place; but this custom has many disadvantages, readily apparent and too numerous to mention.

It was decided to raise the Ninety Six Decennial Memorial Fund by annual subscriptions from the class, so that the giving of small amounts each year might be less arduous financially than the donation of a large sum at the time of the Tenth Reunion. The experiment is proving successful, as is shown by the following statement, which is respectfully submitted by the class secretary.

Those members who for any reason have not yet promised a subscription, are asked to do so as soon as possible. Our class being the largest that ever entered Princeton, should be able to make even a better showing in this respect than it has so far done.

RECEIPTS.

First Instalments, due April 1, 1897, paid...	$363.50	
Second Instalments, due April 1, 1898, paid.	10.75	
Interest on temporary loan to class.........	2.95—	$377.20

EXPENSES.

Temporary loan to class....................	$149.25	
Postage, stationery and printing for Memorial Fund.............................	28.25	
Memorials for deaths of members of class..	12.00	
	$189.50	
Cash on hand March 4, 1898..............	187.70—	$377.20
Amount subscribed yearly for ten years		$509.50
Amount still unpaid on first instalment..............		146.00
Number of subscribers (331 in class)................		120

The following men are subscribers to the fund: Alford, F. O. Allen, Atkinson, Baker, Bennett, Bostwick, Bressler, M. Brien, B. Brien, Bush, Byington, Cadwalader, P. A. Chamberlain, Churchman, Clay, Cochran, Coulter, Dangerfield, A. D. Davis, S. B. Davis, Delafield, Dennis, Dickerman, Dickson, Doolittle, Elliott, Erdman, Evans, Fentress, Fisher, Ford, Fordyce, Galt, T. L. Gaskill, N. B. Gaskill, Glenn, Graham, E. Gray, L. H. Gray, W. K. Greene, Gunster, Hamilton, Hammill, Harkness, Helm, Hodge, Hoffman, Homans, Hoyt, Humes, Jamison, G. Johnston, C. M. Johnson, Judson, Kerr, R. R. Knight, Kurtzeborn, Lampe, Lea, F. C. Leas, L. P. Leas, Litch, Little, Loetscher, Lybyer, McFarlan, McGregor, McGuire, McLanahan, McLain, McMullen, Marvin, Mather, Mattingly, Milbank, F. L. Mills, Moment, Morgan, Morris, Musser, Myers, Newman, Okey, Outhwaite, Parsons, T. E. Pierce, J. Potter, W. W. Potter, Randolph, Reed, Righter, Rives, Roberts, Rogers, Scheide, Schoonmaker, Sherriff, Sinnickson, R. B. Smith, R. D. Smith, Smithers, Sowers, Talmage, Tillinghast, Tower, Trumbull, Ure, Van Syckel, Verner, F. H. Ward, D. E. Warner, Waterhouse, Waters, C. A. Wilson, Willock, Winter, Womack, Worcester.

Reunions.

❧

UR First Reunion was held at the time of the Sesquicentennial Celebration, October 20th to 22d, 1896. Our class being in point of numbers Princeton's foremost class, it occasioned no surprise that Ninety Six had more Alumni back than any other class. The register showed an attendance of about one hundred and seventy-five men. The class headquarters were on Witherspoon street, and were constantly crowded with the returning members of the class. Princeton was filled to overflowing with visitors, but the town offered so many unusual holiday ceremonies and festivities, that there were few opportunities for unity of demonstration as a class. In the Alumni Procession we were given the post of honor as rear guard, and after a long parade around town, sat down to a supper at the headquarters, after which the farewells were said.

In June, 1897, there was a second reunion at Commencement time, at which about eighty-five men were present. The only general gathering of the class was on the day of the Yale game, when we attended the game in a body, entering the varsity grounds in solemn state, preceded by the "Spoon Street" Cadet Band.

Last fall, there was a very informal reunion on October 30th, the day of the game with Dartmouth. The object in holding a reunion on that particular occasion was to avoid the separation that necessarily occurs when a class reunion is held at the time of important athletic events or college festivities of any sort. The reunion was an experiment, and a successful one, there being about fifty men present. The class attended the football game *en masse*, and in the evening met at the *Princetonian*

46

office, where a procession was formed. Most of the men in line were somewhat transformed in appearance, owing to the use, as overcoats. of pajamas and kindred articles of apparel, and to the further disguise afforded by theatrical paint and false beards, which were tastefully distributed about our faces by the trained hands of some members who had once been shining lights of the Triangle Club. The "Spoon Street" orchestra was again in evidence, heading a parade that wandered around "the burgh" for two or three hours, giving the residents a treat and calling on the President and the Dean, who made speeches of welcome. The reunion was voted "good horse," though detracting from our graduate dignity!

Next June the class will have a reunion similar to last year's, at which the activity of the class as a unit will be confined to a parade to the Yale game and to any impromptu celebrations that may then be decided upon. The class will meet at the headquarters in Dickinson Hall on the day of the Yale game at one o'clock. There will be no general assessment to cover the slight expenses of the reunion, which can be met by "taking a collection" from the members present.

Necrology.

EDWARD J. HERRING,
>*Died November 6, 1892.*

HADLEY WYMAN,
>*Died May 2, 1893.*

ERNEST CLAUDE HERR,
>*Died July 1, 1893.*

CHARLES BORLAND STEWART,
>*Died January 6, 1894.*

SYDNEY SERRILL BUNTING,
>*Died February 20, 1897.*

HARRY BEAM CAMPBELL,
>*Died October 16, 1897.*